Robert Burns

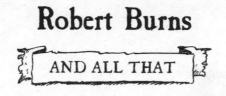

AND ALL THAT

Mrs Hare

Robert Burns

AND ALL THAT

Allan Burnett

Illustrated by Scoular Anderson

BIRLINN

First published in 2007 by
Birlinn Limited
West Newington House
10 Newington Road
Edinburgh
EH9 1QS

www.birlinn.co.uk

ISBN13: 978 1 84158 573 4
ISBN10: 1 84158 573 4

British Library Cataloguing-in-Publication Data
A catalogue record for this book is available from the British Library

Designed by James Hutcheson
Typeset by Iolaire Typesetting, Newtonmore
Printed and bound by Cox & Wyman Ltd, Reading

Contents

Epilogue

Prologue

Darkness fell on the village of Alloway as a fierce storm began pounding the residents' windows and doors. Inside a low, clay cottage a terrified mum prayed for the gale to blow over before any harm came to her newborn son.

Suddenly, a gust of wind slammed into the end of the house. The thick thatched roof was ripped apart like paper. Clay and rocks tumbled over the fireplace in a cloud of smoke and stoor as the baby's mum held him tight.

While the tempest howled angrily through the gaping hole above, the baby's dad rushed over to gather his exhausted wife and their son into his arms. Then, before the walls crashed down and flattened them like tattie scones, the couple ran for all their lives.

It's just as well they did, otherwise you wouldn't be holding this book now.

This story is about what happened to that little baby boy after he was rescued on that stormy night in January 1759. He grew up to lead a very adventurous life, full of excitement and romance. More importantly, he became one of the most famous poets in the world. Perhaps the most famous of all. His name is Robert Burns.

In fact, Burns is the only writer whose birthday is celebrated with a party every year by people all over the globe. It's called Burns Night.

Why do people celebrate Burns Night? Because Robert Burns was brilliant. And the stuff he wrote is still brilliant. His poems, songs and ballads can make you laugh. They can make you cry. They can make you angry. They can make you delighted. They will inspire you, infuriate you, tickle you and make you feel really alive.

Burns wrote poems about mice, lice and witches. And he wrote poems about romance, roses and God.

But mostly Burns wrote about people. Boys and girls. Women and men. Young and old. Good and bad. Scots, English, Irish, French, Americans . . . you name it.

And he had amazingly huge sideburns that bristled on either side of his twinkling, dark eyes. A very handsome fellow he was, too. A big hit with the lassies.

If Burns were still around, he would see that tumblers of whisky are raised in a toast to the lassies every year on Burns Night. And everybody at the party dresses up in kilts and tartans.

The main dish at a Burns Supper is, of course, HAGGIS. A great big, steaming pudding made from blood and guts. Mmmm!

But did Burns ever actually *eat* haggis himself? And did he really wear tartan or a kilt? In fact, did he even like whisky?

Well, let's find out . . .

1

Rantin' Rovin' Robin

Our story begins with Robert's dad, Mr Burns. Mr Burns was a very religious man who didn't like laughter or dancing.

Doesn't sound like much fun does he? But he must have had something going for him since he managed to convince a pretty young woman called Agnes Broun to marry him in 1757.

Maybe Mr Burns had a good job? Well, let's think – he was bossy, dour and not much of a people person. So what did Mr Burns do for a living?

A. He was a teacher
B. He was Homer Simpson's boss
C. He was a gardener
D. He made cheese

Well, he wasn't 'A'. (Although that was a good guess.) And he can't have been 'B' either, because our Mr Burns didn't have yellow skin. In fact, our Mr Burns was both 'C' *and* 'D'.

William Burns, to give him his full name, worked in Edinburgh as a gardener. Then he moved to Alloway and married Agnes, the daughter of a local farmer. Alloway is in a district called Kyle, which is in a part of Scotland called Ayrshire. There, William and Agnes were married and they set up a farm with their own cheese-making business.

William and Agnes kept a dairy herd, whose milk was turned into cheese. In fact, although William was in charge, he often went out to tend rich folk's gardens – and left most of the actual cheese-making to Agnes.

Ayrshire is still famous for its cheese. But, as you have already discovered, it's even more famous for something else. William and Agnes's first child – the hero of our story.

Robert Burns was born on 25 January 1759 in, as we have learned, the Burns family cottage.

Burns's dad had built the house himself. It had thick walls made from clay, small windows, a kitchen, a living room with fireplace and a room for the animals. That's right – the animals lived in the house with the people.

The animals made the place a bit smelly and noisy, but that's what folk were used to back then. This type of cottage was called a 'but and ben', or a 'byre house'.

The family slept in small box beds, one of which was in the kitchen. There was barely enough room to swing a cat. Not that wee Burns would ever have done such a cruel thing to a cat. He liked animals, as we will soon discover.

Anyway, the real trouble with the house wasn't its size. It was that Burns's dad wasn't much of a builder. This meant the house was not put up right.

After a while, one side started to sink into the ground, which made the whole house very shoogly. When that fierce January storm hit, the house didn't stand a chance.

Now, would you want to move back into a cottage that's just collapsed around your ears? No, neither would I.

But Burns's dad had other ideas. Even though the place was clearly on very shaky foundations, he quickly fixed it up again after the storm – and the family lived there for another seven years!

In fact, Burns's wee brother, Gilbert, was born in the cottage in 1760. He was followed by sisters Agnes and Arabella a few years later.

Although Burns's parents were blessed with a few children, they were not so lucky when it came to money. They didn't have much of that.

As a result, wee Burns and his siblings had pretty crummy food. They ate mostly oatmeal and milk.

Now, there's nothing wrong with oatmeal and milk – except when it's *all* you have to eat.

At least Burns's dad made sure his sons got a good education. They were sent to a tutor called John Murdoch. Mr Murdoch didn't teach his pupils exciting stories about Vikings or Egyptian Mummies. Instead, he gave Burns a copy of the Bible, an English grammar book and a spelling book.

Mr Murdoch also taught Burns poetry and songs. But he thought Burns had a terrible singing voice.

Enough, Rab! Your voice is untuneable!

Mr Murdoch had clearly no idea that Burns would grow up to be a songwriting genius!

Burns loved to read, especially about famous heroes like Hannibal who fought the Roman Empire – or the great Scottish warrior, William Wallace.

Burns roved around the neighbourhood on mini-adventures of his own. He later wrote a song about all his ranting and roving. The chorus went like this:

Robin was a rovin' boy,
Rantin', rovin', rantin', rovin',
Robin was a rovin' boy,
Rantin', rovin' Robin!

So who was Robin? He was Burns, of course. Burns had several nicknames in his life, but Robin was his first one. We'll discover some of his other nicknames later.

Anyway, Mr Murdoch had something nasty up his sleeve to make sure Burns – or 'Robin' – never got too carried away with ranting or roving when he was supposed to be in class or doing his homework. It was a leather belt – and Burns got a few lashes when he misbehaved. Ouch!

But the belt wasn't the only thing that made Burns's life painful . . .

2

To A Mouse

When he wasn't studying, Burns had to work on the family farm. It was backbreaking stuff. Coupled with Burns's poor diet, this hard toil was storing up serious health problems for his later life.

Take ploughing, for example. This was done in spring to prepare the ground before sowing the seeds that would grow into crops. You had to use a horse-drawn plough, which was hard on the horse and really hard on the person driving the plough.

At least ploughing had a good effect on young Burns's imagination, because he began to dream about songs and poems as he worked in the fields. In fact, ploughing inspired one of his best poems, which he wrote down years later.

It's called 'To A Mouse'. Here's the first verse:

Wee, sleekit, cowrin',
tim'rous beastie,
O, what a panic's
in thy breastie!

Thou need na start awa sae hasty, wi' bickering brattle! I wad be laith to rin an' chase thee Wi' murd'ring pattle!

So what does it mean? Well, it basically says, 'Hey there, you wee, sleek, frightened creature. What's the panic? There's no need to run away. I'm not going to chase you with my plough!'

The whole poem is about the day Burns accidentally drove his plough through a mouse's house, which was made from leaves and stibble (which means short plant stalks). The mouse ran away in terror and Burns felt bad.

Big deal, you might say. Who cares about a sleekit wee beastie like a mouse? Surely there are more interesting things to write poetry about, like battleships or mysterious murders – or even chocolate biscuits?

Perhaps. But Burns had a big interest in that wee mouse. When he accidentally wrecked its house, he realised human beings can be very destructive towards animals. And Burns didn't believe that was right. He thought people should live in harmony with nature.

So Burns was a bit of an environmentalist. He would probably be appalled if he could see how many animals have become extinct nowadays because of what people have done to the environment – not to mention all the pollution and global warming!

There was another big reason why Burns wrote 'To A Mouse'. He wanted to show that just as the mouse's plan to make a nice home for itself had been suddenly ruined, likewise human plans and schemes can end in disaster – and often there's not a lot we can do about it.

Try as we might to make sure things turn out for the best, they can still sometimes end up in a mess. Or as Burns put it:

> The best laid schemes o' mice an' men
>   Gang aft a-gley,
> An' lea'e us nought but grief an' pain
>   For promis'd joy.

Besides ploughing, and thinking about poems about ploughing, there was even harder work to do later in the year, at harvest time. This was because crops had to be harvested by hand.

CROPS WERE CUT WITH A SCYTHE... ...OR SICKLE... ...THEN STACKED IN STOOKS TO DRY...

... THE GRAINS WERE SEPARATED FROM THE BITS YOU DIDN'T USE – THE STALKS AND CHAFF

HEAVY GRAINS STAY IN BASKET

CHAFF BLOWS AWAY

Burns wrote a lot of poems about life on the farm and many of them were brilliant, especially because they talked about the bad side of farming life as well as the good side.

But thinking about poems made Burns absent-minded while he was working in the fields. Often, he would forget to unload carts of manure for fertilising the ground because he was too busy staring into space, thinking up a new poem. Other people had to complain about the smell before he snapped out of it.

Burns's daydreaming could even be dangerous – especially if he was holding a sharp scythe and swinging it about!

Some people might blame Burns's mum for his head being in the clouds. She sang as she worked in the fields and when Burns heard her singing it put him in a trance.

But although young Burns picked up musical ideas from his mum, he wasn't all that close to her. There was another woman in his life that he was more fond of. And she told him some AMAZING songs and stories . . .

3

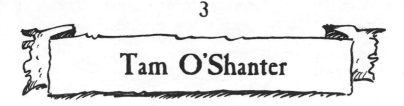

Tam O'Shanter

Burns heard incredible tales and songs from one of his relatives, Betty Davidson. Betty lived with Burns's family and helped out on the farm. She talked about ghosts, giants, witches and enchanted towers – plus a few other things you might not have heard of before:

Apparitions – ghosts who make surprise visits
Bogles – really ugly and frightening supernatural creatures
Broonies – friendly goblins   Carlins – old witches
Cantraips – magic spells   Houlets – owls
Dragouns – dragons – deadly ones!
Elf-candles – flashes of light caused by a supernatural creature like an elf
Faeries – fairies   Kelpies – demons that haunt rivers and try to drown passers-by

Spunkies – goblins that come out in bad weather and lure travellers to their doom

Warlocks – Wizards Who work for the Devil

Wraithes – ghosts of people who are still alive

Betty's weird, wild and wonderful stories got the wheels of Burns's imagination turning. In fact, Burns later said it was Betty's stories that really inspired him to become a poet. He also admitted they gave him nightmares and made him afraid of the dark!

Betty's tales gave Burns the idea for one of his very best poems, which he wrote years later, in 1790.

It's called 'Tam O'Shanter', and the story goes like this . . .

WARNING!

DO NOT READ THIS IF YOU ARE AFRAID OF THE DARK

MARKET DAY IN THE TOWN OF AYR IS ALMOST OVER...

Baaa!

Baa!

..DROUTHY NEEBORS— THIRSTY NEIGHBOURS — GET TOGETHER IN A LOCAL TAVERN AS NIGHT FALLS.

THERE'S A NICE FIRE ON, LOTS OF BEER AND WHISKY TO DRINK AND GOOD BANTER.

AS EVERYONE STARTS TO RELAX AND GET DRUNK, MANY OF THEM FORGET THEY HAVE A LONG RIDE HOME AT THE END OF THE NIGHT...

...AND THEY FORGET THERE'S A STORM BREWING OUTSIDE.

IN THE MIDDLE OF THE CROWD IS A FARMER CALLED TAM O' SHANTER — A REAL BOOZER.

HE HAS ALL BUT FORGOTTEN ABOUT HIS WIFE KATE, WHO'S ANGRILY WAITING FOR HIM AT HOME, MANY MILES AWAY.

THE TIME IS ALMOST MIDNIGHT — THE WITCHING HOUR IS ABOUT TO BEGIN WHEN GHOSTS AND GHOULS ARE SAID TO STALK THE LAND.

BUT TAM HAS TO LEAVE THE TAVERN TO GET HOME.

HE SADDLES UP HIS TRUSTY HORSE MAGGIE AND RIDES OFF INTO THE WILD DARKNESS.

TAM IS DRUNK AND FULL OF DUTCH COURAGE SO HE TELLS HIMSELF THE STORMY NIGHT ISN'T SCARY AND HE SINGS ALOUD TO KEEP HIS SPIRITS UP AS MAGGIE GALLOPS ALONG.

DEEP DOWN, TAM IS REALLY FRIGHTENED. HE KEEPS AN EYE OUT FOR BOGLES AND OTHER NASTY CREATURES.

MAGGIE AND TAM RIDE PAST THE SPOT WHERE A MAN ONCE BROKE HIS NECK...

... AND A PLACE WHERE A MURDER VICTIM WAS FOUND... AND A BIT WHERE SOMEBODY ELSE WAS HANGED...

WHEN THE BOOZY HORSEMAN ARRIVES AT THE GRAVEYARD OF KIRK ALLOWAY...

Gulp!

... HE CAN'T BELIEVE HIS BLEARY EYES...

HE SEES WARLOCKS PLAYING BAGPIPES AND FIDDLES WHILE WITCHES DANCE A WILD REEL...

...AND AT THE CENTRE, AULD NICK — THE DEVIL HIMSELF — IN THE SHAPE OF A HORRIBLE BEAST...

THEN TAM GLIMPSES A WINSOME WENCH — A VERY BONNY LASSIE — JUST LIKE THE BARMAID IN THE TAVERN.

SHE'S WEARING A SHORT DRESS — A CUTTY SARK — AND DANCING WITH THE WITCHES.

ALTHOUGH TAM IS TERRIFIED, HE CAN'T TAKE HIS EYES OFF HER. HE GETS SO EXCITED, HE FORGETS HIMSELF AND CALLS OUT TO HER...

Weel done, Cutty Sark!

SUDDENLY... EVERYTHING IS SILENT. TAM IS IN BIG TROUBLE!

UH-OH!

HE TURNS MAGGIE ON HER HOOF AND GALLOPS AWAY BUT THE DEVIL AND HIS CREW SWARM AFTER HIM LIKE ANGRY BEES.

21

THE TERRIFIED TAM SUDDENLY REMEMBERS THAT WITCHES AND WARLOCKS CANNOT CROSS WATER, SO HE HEADS FOR THE BRIDGE OVER THE RIVER.

TAM AND MAGGIE CROSS THE WATER JUST IN TIME – WELL, ALMOST – A WITCH MANAGES TO CATCH HOLD OF MAGGIE'S TAIL, WHICH COMES AWAY IN HER HAND.

WHEN HE GETS HOME, TAM HAS SOME EXPLAINING TO DO...

There were all these witches...

So the next time you think about staying out with your pals instead of returning home at a sensible time, remember Tam O'Shanter's lucky escape – and ALWAYS GO HOME BEFORE IT GETS TOO LATE!

4

Handsome Nell

You might think these scary stories would have made Burns afraid to chase pretty lassies. No way, not Burns. But before he was old enough to start kissing girls, he had a bit more growing up to do.

After Burns's wee sisters were born, the cottage and land at Alloway weren't big enough for the family. So Burns's dad bought a new farm called Mount Oliphant. The new place was south-east of Alloway. For the next eleven years, Mount Oliphant was home.

It wasn't the best place to live. In fact, it was a bit rubbish. The soil was poor and stony, and the farm was in a lonely spot.

Burns and Gilbert now had to walk two miles to Alloway for their lessons with Mr Murdoch. But at least the walk gave Burns lots of things to look at and think about, and he sometimes met people on the road for a chat.

Burns often spent his evenings with his nose in a book. One that made a big impression on him was called *The Poems of Ossian*, which was said to be a collection of epic stories about ancient Gaelic warriors. The words painted dramatic scenes filled with emotions – like peace, anger, happiness and sadness. Ossian was a 'bard' – a poet who told the world about the history of his people.

But it would be a long time before Burns could think seriously about becoming a full-time poet. In the meantime, there was too much work to do on the farm.

By the time he was fifteen, Burns was the farm's principal labourer. That means he did most of the work. The farm used to have grown-up servants, but there was no money for that now.

So Burns's teenage years were very hard. Now, as we all know, teenagers these days are always moaning that they are hard done by and often get very grumpy.

But Burns really was hard done by. When he wrote later that being a teenager combined 'the cheerless gloom of a hermit with the unceasing moil of a galley slave', he meant it!

All that hard labour made it difficult for Burns to cope with being stressed out. As he got older, he struggled with dark and gloomy moods.

But if there was one thing that could snap Burns out of his depression, it was *romance*. And he got his first taste of that when he was still fifteen.

Burns fell in love with a lass who worked beside him on the farm and helped him take in the harvest. Her name was Nelly Kirkpatrick, or 'handsome Nell', as he liked to call her. Burns wrote a poem about her:

> Once I lov'd a bonnie lass,
> Ay, and I love her still;
> And whilst that virtue warms my breast,
> I'll love my handsome Nell.

After courting handsome Nell for a while, Burns was sent away in summer 1775 to a place called Kirkoswald in Carrick to improve his education. Carrick, a coastal district of Ayrshire south of Kyle, was the homeland of the legendary warrior king Robert the Bruce – and still a place of dangerous adventures.

Smugglers and pirates brought booze, tobacco and other treasures into the hidden coves and inlets around Carrick's coast. Being a curious lad, Burns met some salty characters there and got into all kinds of scrapes.

Plus there were more girls. So Carrick gave Burns a taste of the wild side of life, away from the watchful eyes of his dad.

But the adventure was cut short when Burns was called back to his dad's farm in the midst of an emergency. A new rent collector, or factor, was on the scene. He was a mean, nasty creep, and he had put up the rent on the farm to a level Burns's dad simply couldn't afford. So young Burns's help was needed to try to make ends meet.

This made young Burns very upset and got him thinking about how unfair the world was on poorer people. Our hero was starting to become an angry young man with lots of strong ideas.

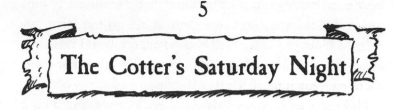

5

The Cotter's Saturday Night

Burn's hot-headedness got him in trouble in 1777, after the wicked factor at Mount Oliphant became so greedy the family was forced to move. They went north to a new farm called Lochlie in the parish of Tarbolton.

Although Lochlie was not as cripplingly expensive as the old place, the soil was sour and difficult. A bit like Rob's relationship with his dad.

Burns had seen how his dad was at the mercy of more powerful people, like factors and landlords, which made Burns think (wrongly) that his dad was a weakling. Burns quickly became a teenage rebel.

To be fair, Burns was not a kid any more. He was almost nineteen, itching to do anything that would help him forget the drudgery and boredom of life on the farm.

Even though Burns's dad was dour and overly religious at times, deep down Burns still loved and respected him. He even wrote one of his best poems in honour of his dad. It's called 'The Cotter's Saturday Night' and it tells of a typical Christian family get-together.

At the centre of the poem is a father, inspired by Burns's dad, who leads the family in Bible reading, psalm-singing and prayer. When this poem was published years later, it was very popular with rich ladies and gentlemen who loved its homely picture of a peasant family.

But not everyone was impressed, especially an old Burns family servant. She thought the scenes in the poem were just ordinary life and therefore nothing special:

It's naething but what I saw in my ain faither's house every night— and I dinna see how he could hae tauld it any other way!

28

Yet Burns had a great gift for making ordinary things sound extraordinary. He could take a farmer, a mouse or even an insect, and make them the heroes of a great rhyming poem or song.

One of the reasons Burns was able to make everyday things so interesting was because he liked to join them up with high-brow subjects like science and philosophy.

In fact, Burns lived during a golden age of science and philosophy. All over Europe, educated men – and some women – were taking part in an exciting new trend that we know today as the Enlightenment.

The word 'Enlightenment' means knowledge. It was about trying to find the answers to big questions, like:

* I know this one sounds daft, but one eccentric Scottish gentleman really believed boys and girls had tails. Burns will meet him later in our story, so keep a lookout.

Scotland had its own Enlightenment. It produced lots of men of genius, who came up with loads of clever new ideas and inventions.

Ordinary folk could join in the Scottish Enlightenment if they became part of a debating society. This was a place where you could hear about new ideas and discuss whether they were any good or not. Or else try to answer big questions about really important stuff.

Being a bright young fellow, of course, Burns wanted to get in on the act. So he and his brother Gilbert clubbed together with a few other young local men to start up a debating society called the Tarbolton Batchelors.

THE SOCIETY MET IN A TAVERN TO TRY TO ANSWER IMPORTANT QUESTIONS ABOUT LIFE, THE UNIVERSE AND EVERYTHING.

NEEDLESS TO SAY, ANSWERS BECAME FUZZIER AS THE NIGHT WENT ON.

...she's a lovely girl... oh!...

Ah, girls. Burns just couldn't get them off his mind. When he was a teenager, apart from Nell and one or two others, he had been quite bashful towards the lassies. But now that he was a man, Burns loved being around them.

Unfortunately for Burns, his parents didn't approve of his interest in the lassies, the Tarbolton Batchelors or his fancy new ideas. They longed for a distraction that would keep him out of trouble.

Little did they know that their son's troubles were only just beginning . . .

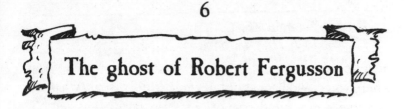

6

The ghost of Robert Fergusson

In 1781, Burns's parents let their son leave the farm to find a steady job, hoping it would keep him on the straight and narrow. He was packed off to the town of Irvine, where he learned how to produce linen from a plant called flax. Linen was woven into cloth for clothes and sheets.

However, sitting in a dark shed and bending over flax plants to rake out the fibres needed to make linen yarn was not Burns's idea of an interesting career. He longed to chuck it and do something he was passionate about instead.

He soon had bigger troubles to deal with:

1 HE BECAME VERY SICK DUE TO A STRANGE ILLNESS AND THOUGHT HE WAS GOING TO DIE. IT WAS PROBABLY RHEUMATISM – A SWELLING OF THE JOINTS AND MUSCLES – VERY SERIOUS IN THOSE DAYS. HE RECOVERED BUT...

2 ... HIS LODGINGS BURNT DOWN AFTER A HOGMANAY PARTY AND HE LOST ALL HIS POSSESSIONS.

Was somebody trying to tell Burns something? Were these brushes with death an omen that his life was doomed to end in tragedy?

Burns found a clue in a local bookshop. There he discovered the work of a young Edinburgh poet called Robert Fergusson. Fergusson had been very good at using the Scots language to write about Scottish life and big, important ideas. Fergusson was everything Burns aspired to be. Except Fergusson had died young, poor and mad only a few years before. Oh dear.

After Burns's life-threatening illness and the fire, it was almost as thought the ghost of Fergusson was trying to tell him something.

'Don't end up like me!'

Then another tragedy struck. Burns was called home urgently. His dad was sick and frail, worn out by years of toil and the stress of paying greedy landlords.

As he lay on his deathbed Mr Burns gathered his children around him – Burns, Gilbert and their five younger brothers and sisters.

And who might that be?

Burns's dad was worried because, as the eldest son, Burns would become head of the household.

Burns's dad died in 1784 and Burns was very upset. But

he tried to show his dad needn't have worried. He moved the family to a new farm called Mossgiel, where the landlord was much nicer, and where they could make a new start. Burns and Gilbert read books on how to be a farmer and learned all they could from other farmers at market.

But Burns's luck didn't change. He and Gilbert still lacked experience as farmers. They sowed bad seed and the next year their harvest was ruined by terrible weather.

Perhaps Burns's dad had been right. Burns had too many fancy ideas in his head to be a good farmer. What's more, Burns's dad had definitely been right about his son's interest in lassies . . .

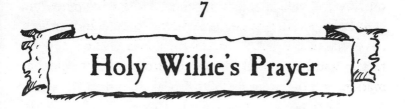

7

Holy Willie's Prayer

With his thick, curly black hair, handsome features and manly figure, Burns was a real head-turner. He stood out especially because he was the only man in the neighbourhood who wore his hair long and tied in a ponytail.

Burns also wore a special plaid around his shoulders that was in a fancy French colour called fillemot, the same colour as dried leaves. Other people wore a grey plaid which looked dull by comparison. And guess what? Women swooned at the sight of Burns wherever he went.

Burns's pal, Sillar, noticed this . . .

But not everyone fell for Burns's charms. There were a lot of stern, religious folk around who didn't approve of the dashing young ploughman who chatted up farmers' daughters.

These self-righteous busybodies were the Kirk elders who helped the ministers of the local churches. The elders kept an eye on what everyone was up to – and punished them if they did anything wrong. The Kirk elders were nicknamed the Holy Willies and they had their beady eyes on Burns.

The Holy Willies could barely hide their delight. In church, they made Burns sit on the stool of repentance – which was a kind of naughty chair. He was attacked and humiliated for getting Lizzie pregnant without being married to her.

Burns's relationship with Lizzie didn't last, but their baby was looked after by Burns's mum.

Meanwhile, Burns got his own back on the Holy Willies using his secret weapon – poetry. He wrote a poem called *Holy Willie's Prayer*, which angrily made fun of the Kirk elders.

O Lord, thou kens what zeal I bear,
When drinkers drink and swearers swear,
And singin' there and dancin' here,
    Wi' great an' sma';
For I am keepit by thy fear
        Free from them a'.

(In other words: other people get into bad habits – but not ME – I am a good, clean-living man!)

O Lord! Yestreen, thou kens, wi' Meg...
Thy pardon I sincerely beg...

(In other words:
I'm a good, clean-living man
... *most* of the time...
but there's this lassie called Meg I really fancy... then there's another called...)

The poem claimed the Holy Willies secretly romanced lassies, too, while they preached to all and sundry that romance was sinful!

To Burns, romance was the most natural thing in the world. How else would the human race keep going? Trouble was, Burns could be reckless and selfish in his romances. Before he knew it, a poor lass like Lizzie was left holding the baby.

But if there was one good thing about the carefree way Burns carried on with the lassies, it was the inspiration it gave him. By now, he was composing all sorts of poems, ditties and songs about love and romance.

Love and Holy Willies weren't the only subjects Burns was writing about, of course. For example, he was also composing powerful poems inspired by his poor family's bad luck and the heartless way they had been treated by rich landlords.

Burns was convinced the world would only be a better place if there were equal rights for both poor and rich people, for the 'haves' and the 'have-nots'. For Burns, this equality was not just a dream, he believed it could really happen.

The proof was in his own friendships, like the one he struck up with his good-natured landlord at Mossgiel, Gavin Hamilton. He was wealthy and collected rents for an earl, yet unlike other landlords he tended to agree with Burns that people from all walks of life should treat each other as equals.

Burns began putting his ideas about equality and romance – including his poems and songs – in a scrapbook. It had an unbelievably long title:

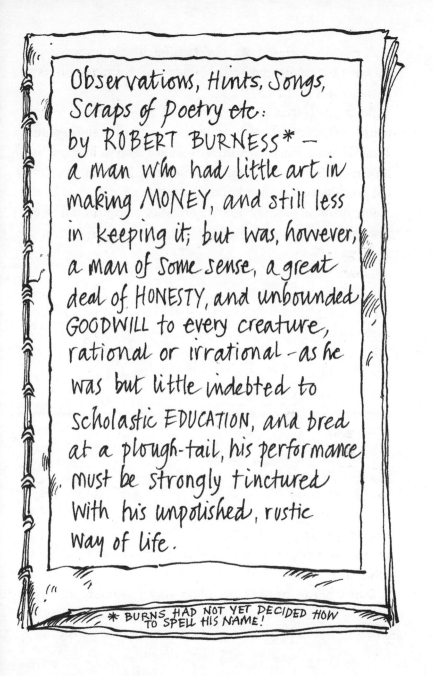

Observations, Hints, Songs,
Scraps of Poetry etc:
by ROBERT BURNESS* —
a man who had little art in
making MONEY, and still less
in keeping it; but was, however,
a man of some sense, a great
deal of HONESTY, and unbounded
GOODWILL to every creature,
rational or irrational — as he
was but little indebted to
scholastic EDUCATION, and bred
at a plough-tail, his performance
must be strongly tinctured
with his unpolished, rustic
way of life.

* BURNS HAD NOT YET DECIDED HOW
TO SPELL HIS NAME!

Snappy titles were not very fashionable in those days. Wouldn't it have been better to just call it 'Robert Burns's Scrapbook'?

Anyway, Burns would soon have to think of better names for his work. Why? Because when he showed his friends his poems, or recited them at dinner parties or in taverns, everyone was blown away by his way with words.

His friends all realized that Burns was a great poet. Even when he wrote about creepy-crawlies climbing all over people . . .

8

To A Louse

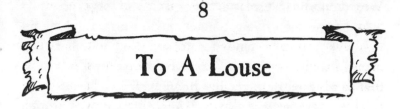

One of Burns's best poems came to him while he sat on a pew at church, watching a louse as it crawled upon a lady's bonnet. The bonnet was a Lunardi, named after a hot-air balloon – a fantastic new flying machine that everyone was talking about.

So the bonnet was a very fancy bit of headgear, the latest fashion, while the louse was just a creepy-crawly from under the floorboards.

And why, exactly, was Burns so interested in this scene? Why didn't he just splatter the beastie and forget about it?

Well, the high-flying bonnet made Burns think about rich folk and their tendency to show off with airs and graces and fancy clothes – or worse, common folk who *pretended* to be rich folk by showing off.

The louse, on the other hand, reminded Burns of himself – a poor ploughman, a vulgar fellow, reckoned to be among the lowest of the low and not much better than an insect.

Burns thought the way the world was divided into rich and poor, high-born and low-born, or upper and lower classes, was just silly and unnatural. So he made fun of it all by turning the bizarre scene in the church into a poem, called 'To A Louse'. It's one of his best.

The young bonnet-wearing woman in the poem is called Jenny, which was probably a nickname for a real girl that Burns knew called Jean Armour. In fact, Jean was to be the love of Burns's life.

Burns probably met Jean in 1785. She was six years younger than him and the couple fell madly in love. By the end of the year, Jean was pregnant.

This was the second time Burns's passion had got the better of him. He knew he was in for it from the Holy Willies, so he came up with a plan.

Over this stream...

Burns and Jean had a private wedding. They didn't tell anybody about it until afterwards, so nobody could try to stop them.

It was a cunning move. Now the Holy Willies couldn't attack Burns because this baby would have married parents. In other words, the baby would be 'legitimate'.

Burns also made plans to leave Scotland and cross the Atlantic to Jamaica, where Britain had colonies that harvested sugar cane and other important crops. Burns planned to earn money on the sugar plantations to make a better life for himself, Jean and their baby.

Unfortunately, many people were not happy about Burns and Jean's private marriage. For a start, there were no witnesses to prove it had taken place.

But, more importantly, Jean's parents didn't want their daughter married to a poor unpublished poet with far-fetched dreams of going to Jamaica. Plus they certainly

...and with this bible, do I thee wed!

didn't want her wedded to a poet with Burns's reputation for chasing the ladies.

Even when Burns promised that he and Jean would stay in Scotland, her parents were having none of it. They even tried to have the marriage annulled, or cancelled.

Burns felt betrayed, angry and heart-broken – but he never stopped loving Jean.

To make matters worse, the farming at Mossgiel continued to go badly. So Burns thought about leaving his misery behind and making a fresh start by going to Jamaica by himself.

Burns had a job as an assistant supervisor on a Jamaican sugar plantation all lined up. It would be a sweet job in more ways than one, but there was only one problem. He simply couldn't find enough money to pay for the ticket to Jamaica. It looked like Burns's dream of a new life in the New World was shattered.

But then his friend Hamilton came up with an idea that could change Burns's fortunes forever. Maybe Burns would be able to buy a ticket out of Scotland, after all . . .

9

Bum clocks and moudieworts

Hamilton urged Burns to get his poetry published. That way Burns could earn some cash while showing off his talent to the world.

Burns thought this was a great idea. He hoped a collected volume of his poetry would sell enough copies for him to afford the ticket to Jamaica.

But there was another obstacle to climb over first. Again, it was money. Getting a book published was a very expensive business. Burns had to pay a book publisher, who used the money to pay for such things as:

1. The paper and covers for every copy of the book.
2. The printer and his ink. In those days, every letter and punctuation mark was on a little block.

To make just a single sentence, the printer had to arrange around twenty blocks in perfect order. Then he used a printing press to put the inky words from the blocks on to the pages. It was a bit like making a potato print, but a lot more complicated.

3. Bookbinders, who put the finished pages and covers together.

So how did a poor young farmer afford all this? Well, the only way to do it was by raising a subscription.

This meant getting people who were interested in his work to promise to buy the book when it was published. The idea was that once all the subscribers received a copy of the book, they would pay Burns and then he could pay his publisher. So Burns had to make sure he raised enough subscriptions to cover his costs before going ahead and getting his book published. And that's exactly what he did.

Burns was helped by the fact that a lot of people in Scotland could read, so there was quite a big market out there for his book. Plus he could let people sample his poems before they decided to take out a subscription. He did this by having the poems printed in special papers called broadsheets.

In July 1786, after enough subscriptions were raised, Burns's first book was published. So did it come with a snappy title? Have a guess what it was called:

A	Of Mice and Men
B	Little Louse on the Prairie
C	Grainspotting
D	Rabbie Cottar and the Philosopher's Drone
E	Poems, chiefly in the Scottish Dialect
F	From Ayr to Eternity
G	Rob the Farmer: Can he Grow it? Yes He Can!
H.	Rhyme and Punishment

The answer is 'E'. Okay, so *Poems, chiefly in the Scottish Dialect* is not the most exciting title, but what did you expect? This was the eighteenth century, after all.

Oh, and by the way, *Of Mice And Men* is a real American novel by a writer called John Steinbeck. Steinbeck was a fan of Burns's poetry and the title of his novel is a tribute to Burns's poem 'To A Mouse'. But you had probably already worked that one out.

Anyway, *Poems, chiefly in the Scottish Dialect* soon had a snappier title. Because it was published by a man called John Wilson, whose business was in Kilmarnock, the book quickly became known simply as the *Kilmarnock Edition*.

As well as 'To A Mouse', the *Kilmarnock Edition* included such poems as 'The Cottar's Saturday Night', 'To A Louse' and 'Scotch Drink'.

Now, can you guess what kind of drink the poem *Scotch Drink* is all about?

A WHISKY B GREEN TEA C PEPPERMINT MOCHA FRAPPUCCINO

The answer is, of course, 'C'. Just hold the peppermint. Hold the mocha. Hold the whipped cream. Hold the syrup. Hold the coffee. Hold the ice, although this bit is optional. Add whisky.

A few words of advice – never let a grown-up drink whisky while they are attempting to read a book of Burns's poetry out loud. Offer them something sensible, like juice or milk, instead.

This is not because Burns didn't approve of whisky – he loved it. It's because the words that Burns used are notoriously difficult for grown-ups to understand these days – even when they're not tipsy!

For example, what do we think Burns was talking about with the words 'lyart haffets'?

A. Lying half-wits
B. Layered half-bits
C. Grey sidewhiskers

Here's a clue – it sounds nothing like the words Burns used. Thank you, that'll be 'C', then. Clear as mud? Thought so.

Lyart haffets can be found in 'The Cotter's Saturday Night', sprouting from the face of the daddy at the head of the family table.

Here are a few more words, from various Burns poems. Try to get your tongue (and your brain) around these:

Moudiewort. You'll find the answer if you dig deep. It's . . . a mole.

Bum clock. Nothing to do with timing your trips to the bathroom. This one's . . . a humming, flying beetle.

Snaw-broo. Drips off the tongue like . . . melted snow.

Baggie. Hungry to learn this one? Mmmm . . . tummy.

Lug. Listen carefully, it means . . . ear.

Auld Nick. Who's party did Tam O'Shanter gatecrash? Say hello again to . . . the Devil.

Auld Reekie. We're going here in the chapter after next. A place called . . . Old Smelly, another name for Edinburgh!

Mixtie-maxtie. By now, you might be getting a bit . . . confused, or jumbled. (Don't worry, me too.)

Ramgunshoch. Trying to re-member all these words is a sure way to make you . . . grumpy.

Sonsie. This is almost the last one. So, a reason to be . . . cheerful.

Ken. Now you've learned all the new words you need to . . . know. (For now, anyway.)

Now, you might be wondering, why the strange lingo? Why not write in plain English? Well, the fact is these words were not strange to Burns. This was the sort of language he and other people across Scotland used every day. They were not peculiar or difficult to understand, they were normal.

The language they belong to is not English, but Scots. Burns did use English, too, sometimes. But he always preferred his native Scots tongue.

Somehow, between Burns's day and our own, most Scottish people forgot how to speak their own languages (Gaelic is the other one). One day, maybe, they will remember.

That would make Burns a sonsie fellow, if he were still around. (Well, actually some folk say our hero *is* still around – but more about that later.)

Anyway, understanding Burns was no problem for the subscribers to the *Kilmarnock Edition* back in 1786. The only worry was, would they like what they read once they took the book home and read it properly?

If they didn't, Burns planned to forget about his dream of being a poet. He would take the money from his book sales and buy a ticket so he could live happily ever after in Jamaica.

But hang on a minute. It seems Burns didn't plan to go it alone, after all. Check this poem out:

> Will ye go to the Indies, my Mary,
> And leave auld Scotia's shore?
> Will ye go to the Indies, my Mary,
> Across th' Atlantic roar?

Who was Mary? And why did Burns want to take her away with him from Scotia (Scotland) to the West Indies?

10

Highland Mary

Burns met Mary Campbell while she worked as a servant in his neighbourhood. Highland Mary, as she was known, was born in 1766 in Dunoon – a village on the Cowal peninsula, northwest of Ayrshire. A lot of legends and stories have been made up about Burns and Mary, but we don't know for sure exactly when or how they met.

Even though Burns had been going out with Jean, and had married her, it seems he also had a thing going on with Mary at the same time!

Burns wrote some beautiful poems inspired by Highland Mary, who spoke Gaelic as well as Scots. One of them was 'My Highland Lassie, O'.

> She has my heart, she has my hand,
> By secret troth and honour's band;
> Till the mortal stroke shall lay me low,
> I'm thine, my Highland Lassie, O!

Burns might have secretly married Mary, too. But he never got the chance to whisk her away with him for a new life in Jamaica. Poor Mary died in Greenock, near Dunoon, from a very nasty disease that was probably typhus. In those days there was no cure, and the illness would have eventually exhausted her body through fever, chills, vomiting and a loss of appetite.

On the other hand, some people claim that Mary's illness was actually caused by a childbirth that went horribly wrong. They also say the baby was Burns's.

Whether or not Burns had lost a baby, he must have been devastated by young Mary's death. So would he just go to Jamaica by himself?

Well, he certainly was tempted, especially since Jean's family still hated him.

Meanwhile,

It looked like the success of Burns's poems would finally give him enough money for a ticket to Jamaica. Yet his growing popularity in Scotland was making him have second thoughts about leaving. He was confused.

Then, in September 1786, Jean gave birth. It was twins – a boy and a girl. Although Jean's parents were still dead against him, Burns realised he didn't want to live thousands of miles away from her and the children. Now he was even more confused.

Burns was caught in a battle between his head and his heart. His head thought he should pursue a sensible career with a steady job in the West Indies. But in his heart he really wanted to stay in Scotland with Jean and the children – and, of course, his poetry. So, before making his mind up, he decided to find out if all the good news he was hearing from Edinburgh was really true. He made plans to ride to the capital to see whether he should try to publish a new volume of his poetry.

A friend lent him a pony and, on the morning of Monday, 27 November 1786, Burns set off. It was the first time he had ever been outside the bit of Scotland where he grew up . . .

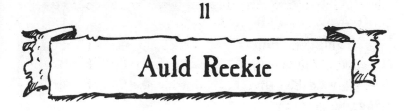

11

Auld Reekie

The journey to Edinburgh was sixty miles long. On the way, Burns kept getting stopped by people who wanted to meet him.

WHEN BURNS ARRIVED IN EDINBURGH HE RENTED ROOMS IN THE OLD TOWN. TALL BUILDINGS LINED THE ROYAL MILE, THE STREET WHICH LED UP TO THE CASTLE.

BURNS SOON FOUND OUT WHY EDINBURGH WAS KNOWN AS 'AULD REEKIE' - OLD SMELLY. SMOKE BILLOWED FROM HUNDREDS OF CHIMNEYS AND FARM ANIMALS WANDERED THROUGH THE NARROW WYNDS. AT CERTAIN TIMES OF DAY, CITIZENS WERE ALLOWED TO EMPTY THEIR CHAMBER POTS. THEY WOULD CALL OUT 'GARDY LOO!' (WATCH OUT FOR THE WATER!) THEN EMPTY THE SMELLY POTS INTO THE STREETS BELOW.

THE 'CROWN Ó THE CAUSIE' - THE HIGHEST BIT OF THE STREET - BEST TO WALK HERE AWAY FROM ALL THE MUCK!

Gardy loo!

WYND - A NARROW LANE →

Yeuch!

BY BURNS'S TIME, A 'NEW TOWN' WAS BEING BUILT NEXT TO THE 'OLD TOWN'. THE STREETS IN THE NEW TOWN WERE WIDE AND STRAIGHT AND THE BUILDINGS MAGNIFICENT. RICH CITIZENS WERE MOVING THERE AS QUICKLY AS POSSIBLE.

Have you heard about the poet who is in town?

Yes, indeed! I hope to meet him!

EVERYONE WANTED TO MEET BURNS AND PORTRAIT PAINTERS QUEUED UP TO PAINT THE PLOUGHMAN POET IN HIS COUNTRY CLOTHES.

BURNS WAS INVITED TO READ HIS POETRY IN THE ELEGANT DRAWING ROOMS AND LIBRARIES OF THE RICH AND WELL-READ CITIZENS OF THE CITY. HE MADE A BIG IMPRESSION ON A YOUNG TEENAGER – WALTER SCOTT – WHO LATER BECAME A WORLD-FAMOUS NOVELIST. HE DESCRIBED BURNS LIKE THIS...

His eye was of a dark cast and glowed – I say literally glowed – when he spoke with feeling or interest. I never saw such another eye in a human head!

(BURNS HAD TWO EYES, OF COURSE!)

Burns was determined to have a good time in Edinburgh, and he did a lot of partying in the town during the few months he was there. He didn't write much during his stay, but he did write one very good poem – 'Address To A Haggis'. Now what was that all about?

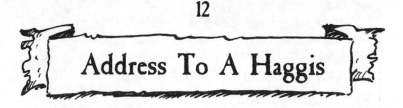

12

Address To A Haggis

'Address To A Haggis' is about a haggis that's going to be eaten. Now, as we all know, a haggis is a mythical Scottish creature with one leg longer than the other so that it can run around the Highland hillsides with ease.

Only joking. Haggis is of course a very old, traditional Scottish meal that's been around for centuries, and possibly more than a thousand years. It has slimy and squishy ingredients.

Don't read the next bit unless you *really* want to know how haggis is made . . .

1 Take heart, lungs and liver of a sheep and boil them.

2 Mince them up with spices, salt, pepper, chopped onions and toasted oatmeal.

3 Take a sheep's stomach and clean it out.

4 Stuff the sheep's stomach with your mixture then sew it up.

WARNING: Don't stuff it too full or it will explode when you...

5 ... boil it thoroughly.

6 Serve it up with mashed neeps and tatties (turnip and potatoes).

7 (Optional) If you don't fancy eating sheep, these days you can buy a vegetarian haggis instead.

Whether it's a meat or a veggie version in front of you, don't forget to read 'Address To A Haggis' before you serve it. The first verse describes the haggis as the king of all dinners, and goes like this:

> Fair fa' your honest, sonsie face
> (meaning: Fair is your honest, happy face)
>
> Great chieftain o' the puddin' race!
> (Great chieftain of the pudding race!)
>
> Aboon them a' ye tak your place
> (Above them all, you take your place)

Painch, tripe or thairm.
(Stomach, tripe or guts.)

Weel are ye wordy of a grace
(Well are you worthy of a grace)

As lang's my arm.
(As long as my arm.)

'Address To A Haggis' is funny but it has a serious meaning. Burns wanted to show that an everyday Scottish dinner, usually eaten by poorer people like himself, was something to celebrate.

Rich people tended to turn their noses up at a gory, poor man's meal like haggis. So this poem was Burns's way of teaching them not to be so snobby and rude about it.

Instead of listening to what he had to say, though, posh Edinburgh types tried to convince Burns to stop writing poems like 'To A Haggis'. They also said he should stop writing in Scots and use the English language instead. Burns politely ignored them.

Sure, Burns was such a master of languages that he enjoyed occasionally writing in English. But Scots was his favourite way of expressing himself. He believed Scotland should be holding on to its native tongue instead of trying to get rid of it!

Again, people in Edinburgh's posh society were amazed a simple farmer like Burns was smart enough to stand up for what he believed in.

One influential Edinburgh citizen who wrote that Burns must have had a special gift from God was Henry Mackenzie.

Mackenzie was one of Burns's heroes. He had written one of Burns's favourite books, called *The Man Of Feeling*. When Mackenzie reviewed Burns's poetry, he wrote that Burns was the 'Heaven-taught ploughman'.

Even though Burns felt he was being patronised, like a child being patted on the head by an adult, he was grateful to Mackenzie for praising his poems. The review created a lot of support for a second edition of Burns's poetry.

While preparations were under way for a new book, Burns got to know some other interesting Edinburgh characters. One of them was a judge called James Burnett, Lord Monboddo. Now this guy really *was* a freak!

Monboddo was weird but brilliant. He wrote an early theory of evolution, long before Charles Darwin appeared on the scene. Some of Monboddo's ideas about evolution, or the origins of the human race, were spot on.

But some of Monboddo's other ideas were barking mad. For a long time, he believed humans are born with a tail!

Burns liked Monboddo because he was eccentric, but also because he held extravagant celebrations like ancient Roman toga parties. Tables were strewn with roses and wine flowed everywhere.

Above all, Burns probably liked Monboddo because one of his daughters was a beauty. Her name was Elizabeth Burnett. Burns wrote: 'I admire God Almighty more than ever, Miss Burnett is the most heavenly of all His works.'

But even though high-society ladies could be heavenly, Burns still liked to get away from them sometimes to enjoy the company of less haughty folk in the Old Town. He joined a drinking club called the Crochallan Fencibles, who met in a tavern on a steep, narrow alley called Anchor Close.

Burns had lots of fun making up verses on the spot, which were often bawdy and outrageous. He loved being

rude about some of the pompous, gentrified people he had met on the Royal Mile or over in the New Town. His bawdy verses went down a storm.

He was also a hit with the lassies of Auld Reekie. He romanced a young woman called May Cameron and soon had another child on the way!

Yet, even though Burns flirted or had relationships with women in Edinburgh, he still seemed to miss Jean. Deep down, he never stopped caring about her.

In April 1787, a brand new edition of Burns's poems was published. It included twenty-two new poems in addition to the ones that had been in the *Kilmarnock Edition*.

It looked like Burns could finally afford to go to the West Indies. But becoming a successful poet now made him much less keen on Jamaica. His heart was winning the battle with his head!

Besides, now that he had visited Edinburgh, he wanted to see the rest of Scotland before going anywhere else. But this would be no ordinary tour of the nation. Burns was on a mission to rescue a musical treasure . . .

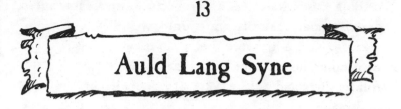

13

Auld Lang Syne

Burns headed for the Borders first. But he didn't ride a pony on this journey. Oh, no. Now he was famous, he got a much fancier set of hooves. A mare.

He named her Jenny Geddes, after a mythical Edinburgh woman who once threw a stool at a minister in church and sparked a riot!

Although Jenny started out on the road stiff and doddery, Burns wrote that she was a spirited mare with a huge appetite for oats. Mile by mile, and oat by oat, she became supple and strong.

Burns also noted that his new horse wasn't much of a singing partner.

He had some strange ideas about horses, but Burns had a sensible reason for travelling around Scotland. He wanted to collect songs. Luckily, the country was filled with them.

People sang a lot more then than they do today. There were no radios, CDs or MP3 players. So singing was the only way to avoid getting bored at work or during the long, dark nights.

But Burns was worried folk were forgetting traditional Scottish songs. Why? Because they were being encouraged to read and write in English. Burns witnessed songs disappearing everywhere he went, as folk struggled to remember words – and even forgot whole verses.

Burns wanted to rescue these old songs before they vanished completely. He thought they were a musical treasure that simply had to be saved. He also hoped they would inspire his own poems and songs.

The most famous song Burns collected was 'Auld Lang Syne', which is sung today by people all over the world.

> Should auld acquaintance be forgot,
> (Should old acquaintances be forgotten)
> And never brought to mind?
> (And never remembered?)
> Should auld acquaintance be forgot
> (Should old acquaintances be forgotten)
> And auld lang syne!
> (And days long ago!)

Burns's search for more songs took him to the Border town of Selkirk, where he pulled up at an inn one rainy Sunday. But, according to one well-known story, Burns didn't find much singing or good cheer inside.

A local doctor wouldn't even allow him a seat at the fire.

The doctor later realised his blunder after somebody explained who Burns was. The doctor was apparently a big fan of Burns's poetry.

The doctor wanted to apologise, but Burns left without giving him the chance. Serves him right for being such a snob, thought Burns.

There was more snobbery in store when Burns returned to the high society of Edinburgh in August 1787. More than ever he felt like he didn't have a true friend in the city, and he became lonely and bored. Plus he still didn't know what his future would hold.

The only Edinburgher he might have been able to properly share his hopes and fears with was the poet Robert Fergusson, and he was long dead! But at least Burns got the chance to visit Fergusson's unmarked grave and even commissioned a mason to give it a headstone.

Burns perked up when he got the chance to go on his biggest adventure yet. Eager to find more inspiration for his poems, he set off for the land of clan warriors and misty mountains. The Highlands here we come . . .

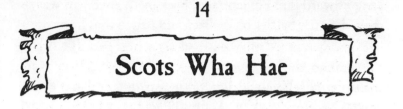

14

Scots Wha Hae

Riding through the Highland glens put a smile on Burns's face. Now he really fell in love with Scotland. As he visited battlefields, castles and other historic sites, Burns felt as though he was travelling back in time.

He visited the field of Culloden near Inverness. This was where Bonnie Prince Charlie's Jacobite army had fought a huge battle in 1746.

The battle was fought just over forty years before Burns visited the place. He heard exciting stories about Bonnie Prince Charlie from older folk who had been around when the Jacobites were on the warpath. Either that or they had just read a book called *Bonnie Prince Charlie And All That*.

Burns collected a lot of Jacobite songs as his Highland tour progressed. The tour also took in places where the Highlands meet the Lowlands, like Stirlingshire.

Here, Burns visited the battlefields of William Wallace and King Robert the Bruce. He remembered reading about Bruce and Wallace as a boy, and how they had both fought to try to free Scotland after the nation was invaded by the English army hundreds of years ago.

Burns went to the field of Bannockburn, outside Stirling,

where the Bruce had fought a huge, bloody battle with King Edward II of England way back in 1314. Burns was so moved by the battles of Wallace and Bruce that he wrote a famous song about the Battle of Bannockburn. It's called 'Scots Wha Hae'.

This song talks about the moment when Bruce is about to lead his brave warriors against Edward II's mighty army. Here are the first couple of verses:

SCOTS WHA HAE
(Meaning: Scots who have)

Scots wha hae wi' Wallace bled,
(Scots who have bled with Wallace,)
Scots wham Bruce has aften led,
(Scots who have been led by Bruce,)
Welcome to your gory bed,
(Welcome to your gory bed,)
Or to victorie!
(or to victory!)

Now's the day and now's the hour;
(Now's the day and now's the hour;)
See the front o' battle lour!
(The start of battle draws near!)
See approach proud Edward's power...
(King Edward and his big army are coming)
Chains and Slaverie!
(This could mean chains and slavery!)

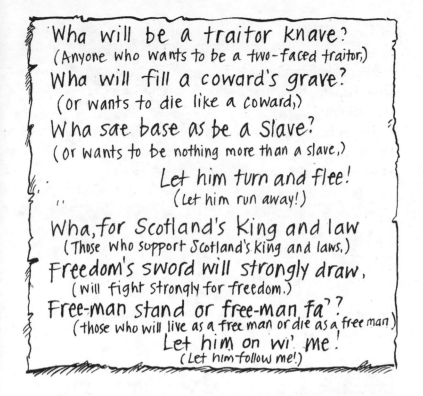

Wha will be a traitor knave?
(Anyone who wants to be a two-faced traitor,)
Wha will fill a coward's grave?
(or wants to die like a coward,)
Wha sae base as be a Slave?
(or wants to be nothing more than a slave,)

Let him turn and flee!
(Let him run away!)

Wha, for Scotland's King and law
(Those who support Scotland's King and laws,)
Freedom's sword will strongly draw,
(will fight strongly for freedom.)
Free-man stand or free-man fa'?
(those who will live as a free man or die as a free man)
Let him on wi' me!
(Let him follow me!)

Not sure what it means? Well, the whole poem basically says the Scots faced three options as they went into battle:

1. Run away. But Burns didn't recommend that. That would make you a coward and a traitor, and chickens always get plucked in the end.

Let me out of here!

2. Fight and get killed. Not ideal, but at least you'll have stood up to that big bully Edward and, for a moment, you'll be free. (That's the moment right before you get skewered by an arrow or splattered by a catapulted rock.)

3. Fight and win. The ideal outcome. Now all those years of misery and humiliation will have finally paid off. You'll have your FREEDOM!

To find out which option the Scots went for, you'll have to read another couple of books: *William Wallace And All That* followed by *Robert the Bruce And All That*. This story's about Robert Burns, so let's get on with it.

Before we go any further, it is worth pointing out that by the time Burns visited these battlefields, the Scots and the English had buried the hatchet. They had learned to live side by side in peace at last, as friends. Which was nice.

Except Burns wasn't convinced the Scots had made a wise move when they agreed to join England (and Wales) in the United Kingdom of Great Britain in 1707. In fact, he thought it had been a really BAD idea.

And, guess what? He later wrote another famous poem about it. It's called 'Such A Parcel Of Rogues In A Nation'.

The 'rogues' were the big-wig, aristocratic Scots who had signed the Union of 1707 – and put an end to Scotland's independence. Why did they do that? Because they all expected to make a lot of money from the deal, one way or another.

As for ordinary Scots, nobody had asked them what they wanted. The toffs just assumed that what was good for them was good for everybody else – and that *really* annoyed Burns.

But although aristocrats in general often got up his nose, Burns still had a soft spot for particular posh people. Especially if they were female . . .

15

Ae Fond Kiss

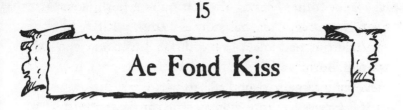

By October 1787, Burns was back in Edinburgh, where he had some important work to do. He was working with a publisher called James Johnson to produce a new series of books.

These were different from the poetry collections Burns had written before. The new books contained the scraps of songs he had collected and polished, or added new bits to, during his tour of the country. The collection was called *The Scots Musical Museum*.

Burns was keen to make trips back to the country whenever he could, especially if it meant visiting his lovely ladies. Besides May Cameron, he had quite a few different romances on the go in 1787 and 1788:

The main romance was with Agnes McLehose. Known as Nancy to her friends, she was quite a posh lady. Burns met Nancy at a tea party in December 1787. She was married but had fallen out with her husband, who lived abroad. Burns's affair with Nancy was a big deal. In fact, he devoted a large part of 1788 to her.

Nancy was a dainty woman who impressed Burns with her knowledge and education. In those days it was very unusual for a girl to be given a proper education. But Burns wished all girls had been taught as well as she had.

After meeting Burns for the first time, Nancy invited him over to her place for tea.

At first, their letters were mostly about the ideas in their heads. They discussed big subjects like literature and religion. But, after a while, they started writing about what was going on in their hearts. Yes, you guessed it – they were falling in love.

'Sylvander' paid secret visits to 'Clarinda' and over time

their letters became very soppy. She told him off for talking about love because she was a married woman – but really she was flattered that Burns fancied her.

'Clarinda' became worried about what people would think of her and Burns having an affair, especially her spiritual adviser – the Reverend John Kemp. Kemp was a stern and dour man who didn't think much of romance.

As time went on, 'Sylvander' and 'Clarinda' began to cool off and they became more like Burns and Nancy again. The letters became fewer, which upset Nancy. She wrote to Burns, tearfully:

> *I wish you had given me a hint, my dear Sylvander, that you were to write to me only once a week. Yesterday I looked for a letter, today I never doubted it; but both days have terminated in disappointment.*

So even in those days people got very upset when the postie had nothing for them.

After a while, the love affair between Burns and Nancy ended. She later went off to the West Indies to find her husband – only to discover he had shacked up with another woman and they had children! So she came back and got on with her life.

Some people don't believe Burns and Nancy ever kissed. That's pretty unlikely, especially given the title of the beautiful poem he wrote to say 'Goodbye'.

It's called 'Ae Fond Kiss' and is based on a song Burns had collected. Here is a tear-jerking bit:

> I'll ne'er blame my partial fancy,
> Naething could resist my Nancy;
> But to see her was to love her,
> Love but her, and love for ever.
> Had we never lov'd sae kindly,
> Had we never lov'd sae blindly,
> Never met — or never parted,
> We had ne'er been broken-hearted.

Sob, sob. Could there be a more romantic poem? Well, yes, there is one. But we'll get to that later. In the meantime, Burns decided he must try to forget Nancy and settle down to enjoy his well-earned success as a published poet.

But things didn't quite go according to plan . . .

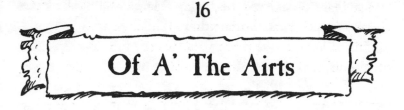

16

Of A' The Airts

Burns should have been on top of the world but he wasn't. His poetry was selling by the cartload. Everywhere he went people treated him like a star.

The trouble was, he was still skint. Penniless. Flat broke. In fact, he had hardly enough money to put a haggis on the table.

But how come? Surely he must have been earning heaps of money from his poetry books? Well, someone was earning loads of cash from his poetry, but it wasn't Burns.

That left Burns with no option but to go back to square one – farming. He found a place at Ellisland, near Dumfries.

Unfortunately, someone else told Burns that by leasing Ellisland he had made 'a poet's, not a farmer's choice'. So what does that mean? Basically, Burns had been unwise – the soil at Ellisland was quite infertile and worn out. It was very hard to grow crops there. This was a disaster for Burns.

But what about poor Jean? After all Burns had put her through, she deserved better. In March 1788, she gave birth to two girls. But neither of the poor wee things survived for more than a few days.

Worse, Jean's parents were nasty to her because she agreed to live with Burns. She even agreed to marry him properly despite the fact he was still having affairs with other ladies. Burns could be really horrible about her sometimes.

Jean's so dull and boring compared to women like Clarinda.

And yet, deep down, he loved Jean more than any other person in his life. They were best friends. They got on. It worked. If only Burns could understand how lucky he was and stop messing about!

Especially since Jean was so patient and loving she even agreed to become the mum of one of the children Burns had had with another woman, Anna Park. Jean once said with a sigh, 'Our Robbie should have had two wives.' Only two?!

What I really want is someone who has Jean's down-to-earth goodness...

... and has an interest in literature, philosophy and all that other clever stuff...

... oh, and she has to be pretty, of course...

... but will I ever find such a lassie?

Enter Mrs Dunlop.

Burns shared a lot of his mixed-up feelings with Mrs Dunlop. He wrote her tons of long letters.

Now, before you get the wrong idea, Mrs Dunlop was much older than Burns and there was certainly no romance going on.

Mrs Dunlop was like a cross between his mum, his teacher and his best pal. She was a wealthy and well-educated woman who cared about Burns and gave him a lot of advice. In return, she was permitted a peek at many of his poems and songs before anybody else.

Mrs Dunlop often gave Burns a row for cheating on Jean. He didn't get angry, but realised she was right. In one volume of the *Scots Musical Museum*, Burns included two songs that complimented his long-suffering wife.

One of these poems was called 'Of A' The Airts' and it was set to a lively type of tune called a strathspey. Here is a bit:

Of a' the airts the wind can blaw,
(Of all the directions the wind can blow from,)
I dearly like the West;
(I dearly like the west;)
For there the bonnie lassie lives,
(For the lovely girl lives there.)
The lassie I lo'e best;
(The girl I love best;)
There wild woods grow, and rivers row,
(There wild woods grow and rivers roll,)
And mony a hill between;
(And there's many hills in between;)
But day and night my fancy's flight
(But day and night my imagination)
Is ever wi' my Jean.
(Is always with my Jean.)

Despite coming out with such upbeat songs, Burns found the tail end of 1788 very difficult to cope with. It was blighted by bad weather, poor progress on his new farm, lack of money and a strange feeling of restlessness.

He needed a change of direction . . .

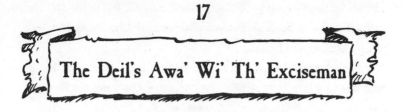

17

The Deil's Awa' Wi' Th' Exciseman

In 1789, Burns decided to take up a job as an exciseman. This was not a popular job, because an exciseman was a kind of taxman. Even though it has to be done, nobody likes paying their taxes!

At least being an exciseman was a well-paid job that came with a pension. It also had a fund for widows and orphans, in case Burns died young and Jean and the kids were left on their own.

Indeed, there was a good chance that Burns would die young, because the life of an exciseman was dangerous. Apart from having to ride for miles every week, which was exhausting, Burns had to try to stop smugglers selling things like rum and tobacco without paying duty.

Burns had a few run-ins with these pirates. He even joked they would be delighted if the Devil turned up and carried an exciseman like himself to Hell. Burns wrote a great poem about this called 'The Deil's Awa' Wi' Th' Exciseman'.

And mony thanks to the muckle black De'il That danced awa' wi' the exciseman...

Yet Burns was so charming he turned out to be a popular exciseman. Or, at least, as popular as an exciseman could ever be!

Things were looking up at last. But there was something about being an exciseman that really annoyed Burns. He had to pledge loyalty to the king of Great Britain, George III. Burns wasn't keen on the king. In fact, he would have preferred it if there wasn't a monarchy at all. And he wasn't the only one.

Kings were growing very unpopular all over Europe. In fact, something nasty was about to happen to the king of France – and it turned Burns's world upside down . . .

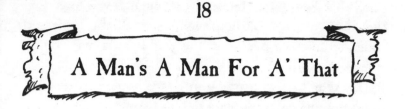

18

A Man's A Man For A' That

In 1789, Burns heard about a revolution in France. He followed the news as the revolution went on and the king of France lost his job. Then things got bloody. Eventually, in January 1793, the king and his family got their heads chopped off.

The basic idea behind the French Revolution was that the royal family should not be allowed to rule the country. So there was no place for kings or queens. Instead, the leaders of a country should be elected by the people.

The French Revolution was bad news if you were the king of another country, like Britain, because all over Europe people were itching to get rid of their monarchs.

One of those itchy people was Burns. He agreed with the French Revolution because he thought it was high time that royalty was abolished, along with all the lords and ladies, so that the people of the world could live side by side as equals.

That didn't mean Burns wanted to chop anyone's head off. Just bring them down a peg or two.

Burns's upbringing had shown him that landlords, for example, could be as greedy and as nasty as they liked, but there was nothing ordinary folk could do about it. So Burns reckoned that to put this right, Scotland needed its own revolution.

Burns wasn't the only Scot thinking along these lines.

After all, these were the days before ordinary people were allowed to vote. None of us had any say in how the country was run. An organisation called the Friends of the People was formed. It's no wonder that revolution was such an angry affair. It wanted change, or reform, so that people *did* get a say in how the country was run.

This didn't please the leader of the Scottish government, Henry Dundas.

When his bosses found out that he supported the reformers, Burns got into deep trouble. After all, his job was to collect the king's taxes! He couldn't afford to do without his work as an exciseman, so he had to write a letter to his bosses stating that the French Revolution was a bad thing.

In later years, Burns also had to keep his bosses happy by joining the Royal Dumfries Volunteers. This was a kind of army regiment, which was supposed to help defend the country against the revolutionaries in France and stop a revolution happening in Britain. Burns kept his true feelings hidden.

Besides the threat of losing your job, there was another reason for keeping your revolutionary ideas to yourself. The British government had passed new laws outlawing the freedom of speech.

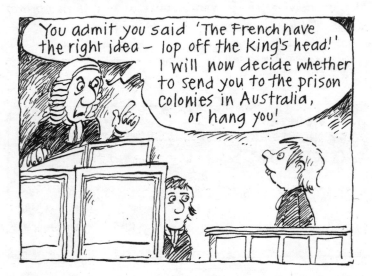

Despite the dangers, in 1792 Burns reportedly came up with a plan to help the revolutionaries. When he stopped and searched a smugglers' ship, he found weapons on board – a set of light cannons made in Falkirk by the Carron Iron Company which were known as 'carronades'. Burns had these secretly sent over to France.

Burns also had other weapons up his sleeve – words. Even though he couldn't say openly what he really thought, he still found ways to express his revolutionary and democratic views in his writing.

When he wrote, people paid attention to what he had to say.

He came up with one of his very best songs around this time, which was all about the idea of democracy. It is called 'A Man's A Man For A' That'.

Athough the message is serious, 'A Man's A Man For A' That' has a very up-beat and jaunty tune. It is also pretty funny in places. Here are a couple of bits:

Ye see yon birkie, ca'd a lord,
(Do you see that guy who calls himself a lord?)
Wha struts, and stares, and a' that;
(See how he struts about as if he owns the place;)
Tho' hundreds worship at his word.
(Well, he might have hundreds of people under his thumb,)
He's but a coof for a' that;
(But he's still a total loser!)

It's comin' yet, for a' that,
(One of these days,)
That man to man the world o'er
(Everybody across the world)
Shall brothers be for a' that.
(Will be equal and treat each other as brothers and sisters.)

The whole song argues that, deep down, everybody is worth the same. Poor people should not cower like slaves under the heels of rich people because being rich does not make you better than anybody else. Great people are not kings or queens, with all their money and privileges. Great people are actually ordinary folk who respect themselves and others.

Some day in the future, Burns believed, people would recognise these facts and put an end to all the poverty and suffering in the world. But the first step was to get rid of titles like kings, queens and lords.

As you can imagine, with the French Revolution going on, this song (sometimes known as 'Is There For Honest Poverty') was so radical it scared some people. It seems crazy to think of it now, but writing about peace, love and happiness at that time really could get you in BIG trouble.

It's no wonder then that Burns sent the song to some newspapers to be published *anonymously* – so nobody in power would know who wrote it. Especially Burns's bosses at the excise office!

Still, Burns paid a price for his radical views. His friend Mrs Dunlop did not approve.

One of my sons is in the army. He has fought against revolutionaries.

By the way, Burns also believed that A Woman's A Woman For A' That. He wrote that girls should grow up with rights and freedoms, too.

He even wrote a speech that stood up for sisters everywhere:

Amid this mighty fuss, just let me mention
The Rights of Woman merit some attention.

As long as revolution fever was still strong, Burns's book editors were too terrified to publish this sort of thing. Especially 'A Man's A Man For A' That'.

In fact, poor Burns would not live long enough to see his great radical song properly published in a book. Actually, it looked like he wasn't going to live long enough to see any democracy come to Scotland either. He was growing very ill . . .

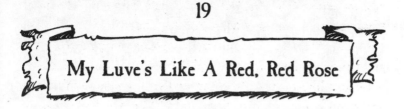

My Luve's Like A Red, Red Rose

While the country was in turmoil and Burns was thinking about the poem that would become 'A Man's A Man For A' That', his personal affairs were not going very well. A lifetime of backbreaking labour had taken its toll on him.

Instead of revolution fever, he had *real* fevers to contend with. He suffered a lot from headaches and other pains, and was often gloomy.

He also gave up on farming forever. So what happened to the farm?

JEAN STRUGGLED TO KEEP THE FARM GOING. SHE HAD FOUR HIRED FARMHANDS TO HELP HER. BURNS HATED TO SEE ANIMALS MISTREATED AND ONCE, THE SERVANT GIRL GOT A REAL TELLING-OFF FOR FEEDING THE COWS POTATOES WHICH HAD NOT BEEN CHOPPED UP PROPERLY.

Do you want the animals to choke to death?

Bleh!

EVENTUALLY, FARMING HAD TO COME TO AN END.

I'm not fit enough for this!

The soil is rubbish – you're wasting your time – there's not even a decent nibble of grass.

BURNS AND HIS FAMILY MOVED INTO A HOUSE IN DUMFRIES – A BIG TOWN WITH A HOSPITAL, BANKS AND A LIBRARY.

THE HOUSE WAS COMFORTABLE AND WELL-FURNISHED. FRIENDS AND NEIGHBOURS SENT GIFTS AND FOOD. BURNS ALWAYS HAD HIS NOSE IN A BOOK.

Oh, Rab, watch what you're doing with that spoon!

After that, his health took a turn for the worse. He wrote letters to old and dear friends saying 'farewell'. He wrote to Mrs Dunlop and tried to patch things up. And he asked his brother Gilbert to look after Jean and the children if he died.

Even though he was on his way out, Burns still had time for the ladies . . .

By now, Burns's rich fans and supporters were finally getting their act together to give money that would help him get better treatment, but they had left it too late.

Burns died on 21 July 1796. He was only thirty-seven years old.

His funeral was attended by an enormous crowd from all walks of life. There were gentry, judges, soldiers and common folk of all occupations. And, of course, Burns's brother and close friend, Gilbert.

A trust fund was set up to look after Jean and the children. There were donations not only from Scotland, but from England too. In fact, more than £700 was raised in England, a very large sum in those days, which shows that Burns was widely loved and admired.

It was just as well a lot of money was raised. Not only had Jean been incredibly loyal and loving to Burns after all he had put her through, she lived on for another thirty-eight years!

Of course, Burns had other children to other women – and they should not be forgotten. In some cases, these children had either died in infancy or were cared for by their mums. Some of them were looked after by Burns's mum or Jean. Others were either given away to outsiders or else we don't know what happened to them. What they all had in common was a dad who was certainly not perfect – he was a loveable rogue.

On the other hand, it was Burns's love of the lassies that inspired him to come up with many of his best poems – poems that have brought huge joy to the hearts of millions of people around the world. Without all his love affairs, they would never have been written. Or, as he put it:

Possibly Burns's greatest ever song was one he wrote while he was gravely ill. It's called 'My Luve's Like A Red, Red Rose'. And yes, you guessed it – it's about romance:

O, my luve's like a red, red rose
That's newly sprung in June;
O, my luve's like a melodie
That's sweetly played in tune.

As fair art thou, my bonnie lass,
So deep in luve am I;
And I will luve thee still, my dear,
Till a' the seas gang dry.

Till a' the seas gang dry, my dear,
And the rocks melt wi' the sun;
And I will luve thee still, my dear,
While the sands o' life shall run.

And fare thee weel, my only luve,
And fare thee weel a-while;
And I will come again, my luve
Tho' it were ten thousand mile.

The sands of life ran out only a couple of years after that song was written and the 'Heaven-taught ploughman' was on his way to Heaven, which is a lot further away than ten thousand miles.

But that's not the end of the story. Burns lives on in the memories of all the generations who have read and loved his poems and songs ever since. In fact, they say the memory of Burns is *immortal* . . .

Epilogue

Since he died, Burns has become a superstar. There are Burns clubs all over the world.

Every year, on Burns Night, people give a speech about Burns called 'The Immortal Memory'. It means that, in a way, Burns is still alive in the hearts of everyone who loves his poetry and songs.

It only took five years after Burns's death before the first Burns club sprang up. It was formed in 1801 in the town of Greenock, where its members recited his poems and ate haggis.

Before long, Burns's work was being published around the globe and translated into many languages.

Today you can buy Burns dinner plates, mugs, coasters, tea towels, calendars, T-shirts, key rings . . . you name it.

You can even buy Burns mouse mats. Now, I wonder if these are for using with a computer? Or should they be put in a field so that a real mouse can wipe its feet before going into its house?

Wee, sleekit, cow'rin', tim'rous beastie!

Anyway, there are lots of ways to appreciate Burns. The cottage where he was born in Alloway has been restored, so you can go and visit it. (The roof's a lot stronger than it used to be!). And concerts are often held celebrate Burns's work.

'Auld Lang Syne' is a song everybody loves because it makes them think of friendship and good times. It always raises a smile.

'A Man's A Man For A' That' has inspired people down generations to fight for honesty, democracy and a fair deal for everyone. It's strong stuff.

So Burns really helped to change the world for the better. That's a huge achievement. It proves words and ideas are really powerful things.

Just think how different the world would be if Burns had called his song 'A Man's A Martian For A' That'. Would we have colonised other planets by now?

Or what about 'A Man's A Munchkin For A' That'. Would that have made us all a lot smaller?

Luckily Burns decided against any crazy titles and today, he and his songs are *still* making history. 'A Man's A Man For A' That' was the official song when Scotland's national parliament was reopened in Edinburgh in 1999, after being adjourned for almost three hundred years.

Now a lot of people believe 'A Man's A Man For A' That' should be Scotland's national anthem. And why not?

Perhaps the parliament could also pass laws in honour of Scotland's national poet. Like making it compulsory for everyone to wear huge sideburns. Or banning farmers from ploughing through mice neighbourhoods.

One law we don't need is one that makes sure people never forget Burns. As long as we keep reading his poetry and singing his songs, the rocks would have to melt wi' the sun and a' the seas gang dry before that ever happened!